BASKETBALL BLOOPERS

WORLD'S FUNNIEST FOUL-UPS

Bill Gutman

Troll

Contents

Introduction

Basketball is a straightforward game. It's played on a court 94 feet (29 meters) long and 50 feet (15 meters) wide. The object is to put the ball through the basket. That's done by dribbling, passing, and shooting the basketball. Defensive players try to force a bad shot, steal a pass, and rebound the ball after a missed shot. It's all basic stuff. Even so, the unusual and the unexpected can still happen.

The sport of basketball is barely more than a hundred years old, having been invented by Dr. James Naismith in 1891. Through the years, however, thousands upon thousands of games have been played—in playgrounds, high schools, and colleges, and into the professional ranks.

With so many games taking place, it's not surprising that strange things sometimes happen. While the average game may go off without a hitch—resulting in a winner, a loser, a high scorer, a hero, and sometimes a goat—there are also games in which something happens that wasn't written into the script. Such unusual court events are often remembered as bloopers, mistakes, or simply errors in judgment. Some of these incidents are funny, even hilarious; others can be frustrating, or even sad, if they result in the loss of a big game.

Basketball Bloopers recounts many of the strange, unexpected, and unusual happenings from the sport of basketball since its beginning. Some of these anecdotes are drawn from the sport's earliest days, when the rules, the courts, and the players were very different from those of today. Back then, college teams often played outdoors—subject to the whims of the weather. Barnstorming pro teams played almost anywhere, from dance halls to basements with pillars, from caged-in courts to courts having baskets with wire backboards or no backboards at all.

The rules that governed basketball in its early days occasionally introduced bloopers. Many such rules remained unchanged until people realized the strange and wacky ways they could affect the maturing game. As with other sports, basketball didn't become the great spectacle it is today without its share of growing pains, crazy characters, and strange moments.

Whether it's an early superstar like Nat Holman putting Vaseline on his shoes to keep from slipping on a dance floor, or Charles Barkley almost eating himself out of a career by ordering two large pizzas every night while in college, or Shaquille O'Neal shattering a backboard with his great strength, basketball has had its share of bloopers.

Enjoy them.

Chapter 1

The Good Old Days
Weren't Always Good

Basketball may be the only team sport invented on request. In 1891 Dr. Luther Gulick, head of the Physical Education Department at the International Training School of the YMCA—located in Springfield, Massachusetts, and later known as Springfield College—sought an indoor game that would interest students during the winter months. He presented his request to James Naismith, a physical education instructor at the school.

The traditional winter physical activities were marching, gymnastics, and calisthenics. Naismith considered bringing some outdoor games, like soccer or rugby, indoors, but he knew that wouldn't work. Gradually, he devised a game played with a large round ball that would be thrown through some kind of goal. Then he nailed two peach baskets to a balcony at each end of the gym. Each basket was exactly 10 feet (3 meters) high. The object of the new game,

Naismith decided, would be to put the ball through the peach basket. He developed a set of rules, and in December of 1891, the game of basketball was born.

Within a year, basketball was introduced at a number of colleges, and by 1898 a group of men were playing the game for pay. Pro basketball had begun, but its early version was a lot different from the game we know today. A look back will not only highlight the game's growing pains, but also indicate how the early game lent itself to strange and unusual moments—bloopers in a sport that was trying to find itself.

Why a Backboard?

In the earliest days of basketball, the game was played without backboards. The basket was suspended on a vertical pole and, later, on the end of a horizontal pole. Obviously, there were no banked shots because there was nothing to bank off. Backboards, however, were not invented to make it easier for shooters. They were created to correct a very obvious blooper.

During early college games in many arenas, fans were able to reach out from behind the basket and deflect a shot as it headed for the hoop. Some people in the audience even used canes or other objects to reach for the shot. While hometown fans probably thought they were helping their team, their interference was ruining the game.

To make the newborn sport more legitimate, a

rule was passed calling for the basket to be attached to a flat perpendicular screen or other rigid surface measuring at least 6 feet (1.8 meters) across and 4 feet (1.2 meters) high. By 1897, most college arenas featured backboards that kept overzealous fans from interfering with shots at the hoop.

Other Backboard Stories

Generally speaking, rules for basketball were standardized for college games before they were for the pros. When a professional in the early twentieth century traveled to play a game, he never knew just what he might find. The trick was to adapt quickly to court conditions, whatever they might be—including various kinds of backboards.

Elmer Ripley, a basketball pioneer and Hall of Famer, remembered backboards made out of chicken wire. They were loose, and the ball didn't bounce back off the board. Today's players wouldn't know what to do with them, but one of the early greats did. Ripley recalled fellow Hall of Famer Nat Holman learning to throw a hard baseball pass right at the middle of the backboard above the basket.

"He'd hit that thing so hard that the ball would stop dead and fall through the basket," Ripley explained.

Holman remembered another kind of backboard. It had glass on both sides and a wooden piece down the middle; moreover, the hoop extended at least a foot out from the backboard.

"With that backboard and hoop it was almost impossible to bank a layup," Holman recalled. "The ball had to go through the net cleanly."

So if a player forgot and tried to bank a simple layup . . . blooper city!

You Call That a Ball?

Talk about a piece of sports equipment making a player look bad. Perhaps the all–time prime example was the early basketball itself. Larger than today's ball and made of leather, it had stitches on one side so a rubber bladder could be placed inside and blown up. It couldn't possibly produce a true bounce.

A player trying to dribble the ball might find the laces striking the floor first and the ball simply bouncing away from him. That wasn't all. Teams often used the same ball for practice that they used for games. Such constant use caused the ball to stretch and lose its shape. No wonder the early pros rarely dribbled the basketball. Since they were never sure where the ball might bounce, many players chose to pass rather than dribble. As a result, some of these pioneer players became great passers, so this blooper had a happy ending.

The Wild Scramble

The first basketball games sometimes looked like free-for-alls, thanks to some odd rules. Perhaps one of the silliest rules was the one regarding a ball going out of bounds. It said that the first player to touch the ball *after* it went out of bounds got to throw it in. It doesn't take a genius to imagine that this led to chaos.

Every time a ball went out of bounds, players from both teams scrambled after it, pushing and shoving each other in an effort to be first to reach the ball. It didn't matter if they crashed into chairs, tables, and spectators. In gyms that had a balcony surrounding the court, the out-of-bounds rule created even more havoc than usual.

Sometimes a loose ball would be batted up into the balcony. Remember the rule: First player to touch the ball after it goes out of bounds gets to inbound. Nearly all the players on both teams would be scrambling up the balcony steps trying to reach the ball. Some enterprising teams even practiced hoisting a teammate onto another player's shoulders and up over the balcony railing so he could be the first to reach the ball.

By 1913, after several years of this madcap mayhem, the rule was changed to the one still in effect today: The team causing the ball to go out of bounds, or the last player touching it *before* it goes out of bounds, loses possession. The wild scrambles were over.

Locked in a Cage

During the early days of basketball, there was a bizarre way to keep the ball inbounds: Use a court that has no out of bounds at all. Believe it or not, many early professional games were played on courts surrounded by either a tight wire cage or a flexible mesh net. Some game historians believe these strange ways of playing basketball began at small armories, where the fans sat so close to the court that they could easily be injured. Basketball fans today wouldn't recognize these games as the sport they have grown to love.

The cage version of the game was rougher than the net game. Players chasing loose balls confined in the cage often banged into and bounced off the wire or—if the cage was reinforced by two-by-fours—off the wood. To soften the impact, players wore hip pads and elbow and knee guards. They looked like football players, and the game they played often resembled hockey. It was, in fact, early basketball.

Playing inside the net had its own problems. The net wasn't rigid like the cage. If a player picked up a loose ball in the corner, the defensive player could grab the net on both sides and pull it around the other guy. The referee would blow his whistle, and a jump ball was called.

The net game could also be dangerous. Nat Holman described the net as being very close to the backboard. Players driving the ball to the hoop would run into the net and bounce back off it. This trampoline effect sometimes caused the driver to crash into the defensive man who had been guarding him, and fans sitting just outside the net would sometimes stick objects through the mesh just as the players were about to hit.

Holman remembered guarding a player named Jack Inglis, then one of the strongest men in the game. They were playing inside the net at a gym that had no backboards. At one point, Inglis cut to the basket with the tenacious Holman sticking to him like glue.

"As we got near the net alongside the basket," Holman recalled, "[Inglis] jumped as high as he could. With his left hand he grabbed the net, pulled himself up, and did a quarter turn right. He was almost level with the basket. One of his teammates fired a baseball pass to him. He caught it with one hand against his chest, and with a little flick tossed it into the open basket."

The cage and net games are long gone now, but at least one reminder lingers: the nickname for basketball players is "cagers." Now you know how it originated.

Crazy Courts

For the most part, college basketball courts weren't too bad in the early days. Once a school began playing the sport, the administration made sure that its team had an acceptable court. It was the early pros who never quite knew what to expect. Many of these pioneers played for more than one team. Since there were no stable leagues in those days, most teams barnstormed, or played wherever a game and a fee were offered.

Where the pros would play next was a constant guessing game. Some of the halls they encountered were suited for many things—but surely not for basketball. In such cases, the pros had to make all kinds of adjustments and just hope the game they ended up playing resembled the one they started out to play.

Nat Holman played for the Original Celtics—one of the greatest of the early pro teams—and had many memories of strange and wacky playing conditions his team had to endure. In Providence, Rhode Island, the Celtics had to play on a court that was surrounded by a 4-foot- (1.2-meter-) high wall.

One of the game's great early pros, the fiery Nat Holman loved the rough play on the crazy courts of yesteryear, including those surrounded by high boards and a wire cage.

14

"When the game started," Holman recalled, "we found ourselves being rammed into those boards just like we were playing hockey."

Holman and other early pros also played many games in dance halls. A basket would be put up at each end for the game, but it was the halftime dance that helped attract paying customers.

"People would drink and dance between halves and the floor would be a slippery mess," Holman remembered. "In places like that we always wore special shoes with holes in the soles. Then we'd fill them with Vaseline so they'd stick to the floor."

Holman played one game at a dance hall where no Vaseline was available. This time the players used kerosene on their shoes so they wouldn't slip. It worked, except for one thing.

"It ruined the floor," Holman explained. "So the next time we played there the owner spread a canvas over the floor with the court markings on the canvas. When we got through playing I could barely walk. The canvas gave whenever we tried to stop short and it just tore up our legs."

Some games were actually played in basement areas with low ceilings. You could shoot a layup but not a high-arcing set shot. Other basement courts included pillars that held up the building. Players soon learned to cut close to the pillars as a way of losing their defensive man. If the defender wasn't looking . . . watch out! A cement pillar is one heck of a pick.

Try This Court on for Size

Although the college players usually had better facilities than the pros, there were some early exceptions. Pioneer coach Ray Kaighn organized the first basketball team at Hamline University, St. Paul, Minnesota, in 1893. To get a game for his ball club, he brought in a team from the local YMCA. When the visitors asked to see the gymnasium, they were led to the basement of Hamline's science building.

This early college court had ceilings that were only 9 feet (2.7 meters) high—Naismith's original rules called for the baskets to be 10 feet (3 meters) high. The teams played, and the boys from the "Y" beat Hamline, 13–12. That must have been some game. Imagine today's players on a court with a ceiling that low. Many of them would hit their heads just going up for a jump shot!

Jet Plane, Anyone?

Today, basketball teams jet from city to city, sometimes cross-country, in a matter of hours. Once they reach their destination, they usually stay in fine hotels. The season is long and sometimes difficult, so their travel conditions are made as comfortable and as easy as possible. Surprise! It wasn't always that way. In the old days, travel was often an adventure. A simple trip to another town or city could be more of a crazy odyssey than the game itself.

Barnstorming pros often had to make their own travel arrangements. That could mean taking a bus, taxi, subway, train, car, or ferry boat—or even just plain

The original Celtics were one of the great early pro teams. These rough-and-tumble guys might not be able to compete today, but today's pros wouldn't want to drive through a raging blizzard in an old car just to get to a game. These Celtics did.

walking. Sometimes a pro played two or three games in one day. Even if they were in the same city, he still had to worry about transportation.

Once, in the early 1920s, the Original Celtics took a train overnight from New York to Michigan. The team had an afternoon game in a town just outside Detroit. Because there weren't enough sleeping berths on the train, some of the players had to sit up all night and were tired when they arrived. They played the game despite fatigue and won. That should have been enough, but it wasn't—not for barnstorming pros who wanted the per-game money.

The team had another game that night in Battle Creek, Michigan, which was about 125 miles (201 kilometers) from Detroit. All seven Celtics climbed into a single car, but almost as soon as the trip began, it started to snow. Soon, the players were driving through a raging blizzard. Somehow, they made it safely to Battle Creek . . . only not quite on time. When they reached the arena, disgruntled fans were already leaving. Because the promoter didn't want to return the money, the team had to stay over and play the next night.

Can you imagine Michael Jordan, Charles Barkley, or Shaquille O'Neal putting up with travel conditions like that?

Watching the Clock

In today's basketball, "watching the clock" usually refers to the shot clock or the game clock—checking to make sure there's enough time to get off a shot or to figure out a strategy for the final minutes or seconds of the game. But in the old days, watching the clock sometimes referred to checking real time on the clock on the wall. It wasn't a matter of winning or losing but of making the train.

Nat Holman remembered playing in Bridgeport, Connecticut, with the Original Celtics. Back then, only one train went from Bridgeport to New York each night. It was important for the players to make the train because they didn't have enough money to pay for overnight accommodations. And many of them had regular day jobs to get back to. It was often close timing.

"We would play our game, throw our sweaters on, and carry the rest of our clothes as we ran for the train," Holman recalled. "Someone got ice cream and sandwiches for the trip back. It was really a trying situation, very tiring."

They Weren't Millionaires

In today's professional game, a good player doesn't think about making a million dollars; instead, he wonders how many millions he'll earn over how many years. Ask a top pro today if he would play a game for $25 and he'd probably think you were crazy! But guess what? That's how much some of the superstars of the early pro games were paid. Some made just $10, others $15, some $25. That's why they would play as many games as they could on weekends. Pro basketball wasn't a full-time job.

Even during the late 1930s and early 1940s, before the National Basketball Association (NBA) began, most players were still making $25 or $30 per game. The superstars of the time earned perhaps $100.

"You were almost embarrassed to tell anyone what you were making," said Matt Guokas, Sr., who played for the Brooklyn Visitations. "If you went home with $30 or $35 in your pocket, it was a big deal."

Another outstanding early pro, Bob Davies, remembered what it was like after he finished an All-American career at Seton Hall. "Guys coming out of college were saying, 'Well, maybe I can supplement my income with a thirty- or forty-dollar weekend just by playing a game here and there,'" he explained.

Even the owners had some strange tricks to try to make more money from the game. According to Davies, "Some team owners might have jerseys for four different teams. One night they would be the Brooklyn Visitations and wear jerseys for that team. The next night the very same players would wear different shirts and be the Jersey City Reds. I don't know if I should call it a carnival operation, but that's just about what it was."

If you asked a player back then what team he played for, he wouldn't answer automatically but would probably ask, "On what night?"

Two for the Price of One

Former Notre Dame Athletic Director Edward "Moose" Krause took the concept of multiple teams one step further. In his pro basketball days, he once played with two different teams in the same game.

"I was the center on two teams one year," he said. "The Boston Goodwins and the Narcus Brothers. Wouldn't you know it, they decided to play each other for the championship of New England. I didn't know what to do. Finally, I decided to play with one team one half and one team the other half."

So Krause was with the Narcus Brothers for the first half, and they took the lead. Then he played for the Goodwins after intermission, and they caught up and won the title. That would be akin to Hakeem Olajuwon playing for the Houston Rockets in the first half, then switching to the Utah Jazz for the second half. Bloopers of that magnitude couldn't happen today.

But back then, it was a different game. Krause also said that neither team gave him a break.

"Both sides beat the heck out of me," he related. "Even though the Goodwins were going to get me for the second half, they still worked me over because they were trying to keep us from scoring so they wouldn't be too far behind when I switched sides."

It could only have happened in the good old days.

Chapter 2

Rules with Built-in Bloopers

Like any emerging sport, basketball had to go through a period of growth and change. Unlike baseball, football, and hockey, however, basketball did not develop standardized rules very quickly. By 1920, the other three sports had settled on basically the same rules that they use today, but college and professional basketball in the 1920s was very different from the 1990s version.

The early rules often didn't do the game justice. They slowed it down, cluttered it up, and prevented it from finding a real fan base for many years. In fact, played under some of the early rules, a basketball game often became one big blooper. We've already seen one example, where the first player to touch a ball *after* it went out of bounds retained possession for his team. That rule led to chaos. Well, there were others. Let's look at how some of them affected the game.

Dribbling Skyward

When James Naismith invented the game of basketball, he overlooked one important element—the dribble. There simply was no provision for bouncing the ball. Players passed it back and forth until someone had a clear shot at the basket. It soon became apparent, however, that if a man was guarded very closely, he couldn't pass. To alleviate this situation, a very strange rule was created.

If a player was guarded so closely that he couldn't pass the ball to a teammate, he could pass it to himself. Sound strange? It was. He had to throw the ball in the air higher than his head. He could then move away from his defender to catch the ball and hopefully have enough room to pass it to a teammate.

The single toss in the air slowly became a series of throws, and before long someone realized it made more sense to bounce the ball. After all, it would look kind of silly to watch a man playing catch with himself all over the court.

The Center Jump

Every basketball fan knows that the game begins with the center jump. The players gather around the circle at midcourt, and two opposing players try to tap the ball to a teammate after the referee tosses it in the air between them. In today's game, the opening jump, or tap, might be the only one you see. It wasn't always that way.

For many years there was a rule that almost

destroyed the game. The rule called for a center jump after each and every basket. What a blooper! These constant breaks in the action stopped players' momentum and slowed down a good game. With a center jump after each basket, there was no way a team could fast-break. What was the reason for such a strange rule?

Many coaches and athletic directors assumed that players couldn't run for most of the length of a forty-minute collegiate game. The center jump, they reasoned, would give players a brief rest after each basket. So while play stopped and the players trudged back to center court for another jump, the clock kept running. Even in the mid 1930s, this thinking prevailed, especially in colleges.

The result was slow, low-scoring games that often left the fans yawning and bored. With the clock running as play literally stopped for each center jump, some nine to twelve minutes of game time were devoid of actual playing. As of the 1937–38 collegiate season, the rule was changed and the center jump after each basket was eliminated forever. Good riddance.

Now, teams simply put the ball in play under their basket after a hoop is scored.

Goaltending Anyone?

One of the biggest assets any team can have is a quick, big man with the uncanny sense of timing that allows him to block shots. There have been many great shot blockers over the years, players like Bill Russell, Wilt Chamberlain, Nate Thurmond, Bill Walton, Patrick Ewing, Hakeem Olajuwon, and Dikembe Mutombo—just to name a few.

Swatting at the opponent's shots, however, is governed by a hard-and-fast rule. The player blocking the shot must get the ball on its way up. Once the ball begins descending to the basket, it cannot be blocked. If a ball is blocked as it descends to the hoop, goaltending is called. That's a violation, and the basket counts.

Once upon a time, however, the rule didn't read that way. A defensive man could bat the ball away from the basket at any point. This did not begin to change until the early 1940s, when taller men were coming into the game. It was becoming increasingly easy for them to stand under the basket and bat shots away. When George Mikan, 6 feet 10 inches (2.08 meters), arrived at DePaul University and Bob "Foothills" Kurland, nearly 7 feet (2.13 meters), began playing at Oklahoma A&M in 1942, the game—and the goaltending rule—would change forever.

Mikan and Kurland were not only big and tall, but they also learned the game well and were very talented. Seeing the future in these two big men, rule makers knew they would have a gigantic blooper on their hands if they didn't change the rule about blocking shots. So, as of the 1944–45 season, a player could no longer block a shot once it started its downward path to the basket.

At 6 feet 10 inches (2.08 meters), George Mikan was basketball's first great "big man." He was one of the prime players who led to the change that got rid of an old blooper rule that made goaltending a legal play.

What's a Coach for, Anyway?

A good coach can often affect the outcome of a game. He might notice a bad matchup, or decide his team would fare better using a man-to-man defense instead of a zone. He might want his team to slow the pace of the game down, or speed it up. During timeouts, he'll instruct the players on what to do next.

Does it make sense, then, that for years a coach

could not talk to his team once the game began? Maybe not, but that's the way it was in college basketball for a long time. Once the game started, the team was on its own. During timeouts, the players just sat on the court, talking among themselves.

There were certainly great coaches then, guys who got their teams ready to play. Once the game started, however, the players were isolated from their coach. Finally, in 1948–49, this blooper was revised. After all, baseball managers were allowed to talk to their teams throughout the entire game. Football coaches were in the heat of the action every down. Why not basketball coaches? With the rule change, they could really show their stuff and make timeout strategy an important part of the game.

The Game That Changed NBA History

Stalling was a basketball strategy in both college and pro games for many years. Some teams would slow the pace of the game when they got a lead. After all, if the other team couldn't shoot, it couldn't score. The best way to keep a team from shooting was to hold on to the ball. Most of the time, the stall would occur in the final minutes of a game. While fans didn't like it, they tolerated it—especially if their team was winning.

On November 22, 1950, however, an NBA game between the Fort Wayne Pistons and Minneapolis Lakers altered the game of basketball. That game took stalling to the limit and nearly put the fans to sleep.

The Lakers were the NBA's dominant team in 1950, largely because of George Mikan. He was the game's first dominant center, and with him in the lineup, the Lakers were hard to beat. But on this November night in Minneapolis, the Pistons decided to try an amazing strategy—a game-long stall.

Every time the Pistons brought the ball upcourt, they stopped just past half court and simply began passing the ball back and forth. The Lakers defense didn't come out to challenge, so the Pistons continued to pass the ball. Scoring was painfully absent, with hoops coming few and far between. At the end of the first quarter, the Pistons held an 8–7 lead. By the half, the Lakers had crawled on top, 13–11.

After intermission, the stall continued. Fans began showing their disgust by showering the court with debris. Yet going into the final period, the Lakers still held a one-point lead at 17–16. Instead of opening up, the game only became slower. In the first eight minutes of the final session, each team could manage just a single free throw. The Lakers led 18–17 with four minutes left. So what did the Pistons do the last four minutes? They stalled again, freezing the ball for a final shot.

Finally, with just ten seconds left, Fort Wayne center Larry Foust threw up a short hook between Mikan's outstretched arms and it went in. Fort Wayne won the lowest-scoring game in NBA history by a 19–18 score. Mikan had 15 of his team's 18 points. The Fort Wayne leading scorer was John Oldham, who tallied just 5.

There was no way to protest the game because no rules had been broken, but the NBA didn't want the stalling strategy to become the norm. Perhaps the Piston's hero, Larry Foust, summed it up best when he said, "It was a stinking ball game, a rotten ball game."

It took another few years, but as of the 1954–55 season the NBA established a rule stipulating that once a team got possession of the ball, they had only 24 seconds to put up a shot or they would lose the ball. That one simple rule ended stalling forever, eliminating another blooper. Colleges took much longer to outlaw periodic stalling. They instituted a 45-second rule in the 1985–86 season and shortened it to 35 seconds in 1993–94.

Basketball as a Walking Game

In addition to stalling, NBA teams in the early 1950s began taking advantage of existing rules to slow the game down another way. Since a basket counted for two points (there were no three-point field goals then) and a foul shot yielded one point, some of the resident geniuses figured it was better to foul a player than to let him take a set shot or jumper, or drive to the hoop.

The intentional foul became a strategy, and then teams began trading fouls. You foul me; I foul you. Sometimes the fouls would be committed as soon as a team put the ball in play. Games occasionally deteriorated into ten players walking from one foul line to another. During a 1953 playoff game between the Boston Celtics and the Syracuse Nationals the foul-trading strategy came to a boring head, forcing the league to admit it needed to institute a rule change.

On one level, the game must have seemed like one of the most exciting contests ever played. It went into four overtimes before the Celtics won, at 111–105, with Boston's star guard, Bob Cousy, scoring a playoff record 50 points. A closer look at the game, however, showed everyone that it had been one big blooper.

The teams began trading fouls almost from the opening tip. When it ended, a total of 107 fouls had been called, with the players taking 130 free throws. Of Cousy's 50 points, 30 came from his 32 free-throw attempts. A total of eleven players on both teams had fouled out. Games like this were not only boring, they were taking so long that the TV stations couldn't televise them to conclusion. Something had to be done.

The following year the NBA instituted a new rule allowing each team only six fouls per quarter. If a team went over this quota, their opponents would be awarded a bonus free throw. Once again a new rule improved the game. Trading fouls wasn't worth the price, so the game speeded up, the fans were happier, and another old-fashioned blooper went by the boards.

The Game That Wasn't Really Basketball

When James Naismith invented basketball, he intended the sport to be played by women, as well as by men. Indeed, women took up the game at the same time the men did. The earliest female players actually competed in long dresses, which made them look like they were going to a formal dance.

Speaking of dances, it wasn't unusual for women's games to stop suddenly and a dance to begin. In the early 1900s at the University of Illinois, for example, women's games in the loft of the Natural History Building were often interrupted. Male students would sneak up to watch the games, and soon couples would be dancing—and basketball forgotten. Because of this, the school abolished the sport for several years. It was a rocky beginning for women's basketball, at least at one school.

The rules for women's basketball made the sport so different from the men's game that it was almost a joke. This bias lasted more than half a century before people realized that women should be playing the same game as the men.

The earliest version of women's basketball was played with nine to a side. Each player was confined to a certain area of the court, and the ball had to be passed from area to area before a shot could be taken. After a few years, the rules were changed to allow six to a side, but the game still had a strange look.

Three guards had to stay at one end of the court for defense. The three other players, the forwards, were stationed at the other end to take the shots. None of the players was allowed to run up and down the court. Not surprisingly, there was also a rule against dribbling. This wasn't unlike the early men's game, but it took a long time to change substantially.

First, the women were allowed to bounce the ball just once before making a pass or taking a shot. By the 1950s, when the men's college game was attracting large crowds and the NBA was in its first phase of growth, the women were allowed a grand total of two bounces. In the 1960s, when the men's game was moving into an era of great players, the women were allowed only three bounces.

Not until the 1970s was the game modified to allow five players to a side and to include the modern dribbling rule. Finally, women's basketball had come of age. Now players like Carol Blazejowski, Lynette Woodard, Ann Meyers, Cheryl Miller, Rebecca Lobo, and Lisa Leslie could show off their talents the same way as the men.

The Alcindor Rule

Of all the rules in basketball's history, perhaps the most ridiculous went into effect as of the 1967–68 season. It shocked both players and fans when the slam-dunk—the jam—was made illegal at both the college and the high-school levels. Officials were so adamant about this rule that players weren't even allowed to dunk during practice.

In the opinion of many people, one player caused this blooper of a rule change. He was UCLA junior center Lew Alcindor, who would later change his name to Kareem Abdul-Jabbar. Alcindor, who was 7 feet 1 inch (2.16 meters) tall, was a talented superstar who had led the Bruins to an NCAA championship and an undefeated 1966–67 season. Operating under the basket, Alcindor probably dunked more than any other player in the history of the sport. Because he made it look so easy, officials figured there would soon be so much dunking that many of the basic fundamentals of the game would be lost.

The rule against slam-dunks took away one of basketball's most exciting plays. Without the slam-dunk to rely on, Alcindor actually became a better

When Lew Alcindor (aka Kareem Abdul-Jabbar) was a college star at UCLA, the dunk shot was made illegal, a blooper if there ever was one. All it did was allow Abdul-Jabbar (number 33) to develop his famed sky hook, the most unstoppable shot in basketball history.

ballplayer, developing his unstoppable sky hook and a variety of other moves underneath the basket. He led the Bruins to two more national titles before moving on to a Hall of Fame pro career.

Even after Alcindor graduated to the pro division, the dunk remained an outlawed shot—and the players missed it. Ray Williams, of Minnesota, who went on to a solid pro career, perhaps spoke for all college players of that era when he said, "[Not being able to dunk] was hard to live with. There were so many times I'd be flying up above the rim, ready to jam, when I'd hear this voice saying, 'No, no, no.'"

There were also times when players would just ignore the rule, slam the ball home, and take a technical foul. "Those slams always felt better than any technical could ever hurt," Williams said.

Meanwhile, at the same time that college players couldn't dunk, the jam had become a major part of the professional game—an in-your-face move that the fans loved. The pros were even having slam-dunk contests. It took until the 1976–77 season for college officials to realize that they had made a mistake by creating an absurd rule. Finally, high-flying players were once again allowed to dunk the basketball, and they've been doing it with flash and verve ever since.

The old rules! It took a while to get them right, but the process helped iron out the wrinkles in the game . . . and the bloopers.

Chapter 3

Growing Pains
Can Drive You Crazy

On the way to the ultra-modern, 20,000-seat arenas of today, complete with luxury skyboxes and brilliant laser-light displays, both the college and the pro games experienced years of growing pains. Despite many great athletes, the playing conditions sometimes turned basketball into a sideshow. At times the laughs came as quickly as the baskets.

All Eyes Were on Texas

There is nothing really unusual about a one-sided game. Call it a blowout, a laugher. It happens. One team will come out and do nothing wrong. At the same time, the other team can't buy a basket. The result may be a 20- or 30-point victory—which is the proverbial blowout.

A few games over the years, however, were so lopsided that it was a king-sized mistake to play them in the first place. One such game took place during the 1915–16 season. In those days, the University of Texas had one of the best teams in the country. The Longhorns were one of the few teams that still played home games outdoors. By the start of the 1915–16 season, Texas was in the midst of a then-record 44-game win streak.

The opener that year was against tiny San Marcos Baptist. Basketball must have been a new sport at San Marcos, judging by the result of the game. In fact, it seems as if no one at San Marcos even knew how to play. When the smoke cleared, Texas had an unbelievable 102–1 victory. This is even more amazing when you consider that most games in the sport's early days were low-scoring. Some winning teams scored only 20 or 30 points.

The Worst Beating Ever

Amazing blowouts due to scheduling bloopers have cropped up here and there over the years. None, however, resulted in a more one-sided game than the meeting between two New Jersey teams— tiny Englewood Cliffs College and Essex County Community College—on January 29, 1974.

Neither school was a basketball powerhouse, but Essex had a very solid team that year, while the Englewood Cliffs program was floundering on shaky ground. The disparity showed immediately, as Essex raced to a 26–0 lead in the early minutes. It just got worse. By halftime, Essex had a mind-boggling 110–29 advantage. Perhaps the humane thing to do would have been to end the game right there.

But rules are rules. In the third quarter it got so bad that some of the Essex players wanted to let up. Then a radio announcer reminded them that they were in striking distance of the single-game collegiate scoring record of 202 points.

"I didn't want to embarrass Englewood," said Essex coach Cleo Hill. "But the kids asked me to let them have a shot at the record, and I said okay."

That was all the team needed. The rest of the game was pure racehorse basketball, with Essex stealing the ball and fast-breaking, stealing the ball and fast-breaking . . . again and again. When it ended, the Wolverines had broken the record and at the same time had won by the most lopsided score ever. The final was 210–67. Amazing as it was, it was not a game that did basketball proud.

The Snake Pit

Basketball didn't really become an established professional sport until the late 1940s and early 1950s. Yet even then, the pro game was experiencing its share of growing pains. The National Basketball League (NBL) didn't have large arenas like those of the Basketball Association of America (BAA), which would later become the NBA. The NBL, however, did have some great players during the late 1940s—as well as its fair share of funny stories.

Hall of Fame guard Bobby Davies remembered a time he and his Rochester Royals teammates traveled to Fort Wayne, Indiana, to play the Pistons. The arena they played in had a 6-foot (1.8-meter) brick wall at one end of the court. It was a tough place to play, and the Royals referred to it as the Snake Pit.

At one point in the game, Rochester's Al Cervi drove hard to the hoop. As he went up for the shot, he ran smack into referee Pat Kennedy, knocking Kennedy hard into the brick wall. Kennedy was injured on the play and didn't get up. Here's how Davies remembered what happened next:

"Because Al was fouled before he ran into Kennedy, our coach, Les Harrison, came running onto the floor. He didn't ask if Kennedy was all right, just started screaming at him, 'He was fouled; he was fouled. Give him two shots.'

"Pat Kennedy looked up from the floor in pain and said, 'Les, don't bother me. I'm dying.'

"And without taking a breath, Les replied, 'Well, before you die, give him two shots.'"

So the intensity was there. Every team wanted to win. Only it wasn't always easy when there was a brick wall waiting to sabotage the game.

Snowdrifts

The Snake Pit in Fort Wayne wasn't the only NBL arena that could cause problems. In fact, the Royals shouldn't have complained about it. Their home court was the old Edgerton Park Arena, in Rochester, New York. The Royals were a top team then, but Edgerton Park left something to be desired. It was a bandbox, a tiny gymnasium masquerading as a professional arena.

In fact, the court area was so small that the backboards were attached directly to the walls at both ends of the arena. That presented a problem for players driving hard at the basket. They had three choices. They could try to stop short to avoid running into the wall. Or they could take a chance, run into the wall, and hope they wouldn't get hurt. Then there was the third—and strangest—choice of all.

There were doors at each end of the arena right under the baskets. The Royals had attendants whose job it was to open the doors whenever a player drove to the hoop. That gave the player the choice of running out into the cold Rochester night. At least he wouldn't hit the wall. But what happened when players went out those doors?

It was an adventure, all right. During the winter months there were often snowdrifts piled high near the doors, and players would run right into them, returning to the game with snow all over their shoes and legs. Sometimes they would run smack into late-arriving fans, leading to collisions that could cause injuries. A player charging through those doors at top speed never knew quite what to expect on the other side.

Eventually, most players decided it was too risky to run through the doors. Instead, they learned to veer into the wall at an angle so they wouldn't get hurt. It was arenas like Edgerton Park that led to the eventual demise of the NBL, with the best teams jumping over to the BAA, which soon became the National Basketball Association (NBA).

It's hard to believe stories like that now, but they really happened. Can you imagine Michael Jordan driving in for a sensational hoop, then having to run out into a snowdrift?

I'm Playing Where?

Today the best college basketball players await the annual NBA draft with excitement. They are anxious to know how high they will be picked, and they want to know where their professional careers will begin. Will it be Los Angeles, Chicago, New York, Orlando, Vancouver? NBA franchises are everywhere. Yet there was a time when a top pro prospect, a future all-time great, actually couldn't figure out just where his new team was located.

Bob Cousy was a senior All-American guard at Holy Cross during the 1949–50 season. Upon graduation, he waited to see which NBA team would pick him. When he received the news, he was flabbergasted. Hearing that his first pro team would be the Tri-Cities Blackhawks, Cousy asked a now-classic question.

"What's a Tri-Cities?" he wanted to know.

Cousy didn't even know where the team was located; a lot of other people didn't, either. The answer was Moline, Illinois, but since the Blackhawks also played home games in two other small Illinois cities, they were called Tri-Cities.

Fortunately, it all worked out for Cousy. He was traded to the Chicago Stags and, when that franchise folded, went on to a Hall of Fame career with the Boston Celtics. As for Tri-Cities, that elusive franchise didn't last very long. The team soon moved to Milwaukee, then to St. Louis, and finally to Atlanta, where it flourishes today as the Hawks.

In basketball's early days some franchises were so obscure that the players didn't even know where they were. If that's not a blooper, nothing is.

When It Was Dangerous to Call a Foul

Some of the old NBA arenas were so small that the fans sat dangerously close to the court. They felt they were part of the game, and they lived and died with the home team. Syracuse was an especially tough place to play. The fans loved their Nationals (later the Philadelphia 76ers) and hated every visiting team.

Would you believe the most dangerous job at Syracuse was being a referee? Sid Borgia was perhaps the league's highest-profile ref in the 1950s and 1960s. Borgia was balding and shorter than all the players in the league, but he controlled a game as well as anyone and refused to be intimidated. At Syracuse, however, much of the intimidation could come from the fans, who were packed close to the sidelines.

One night, the Nats were hosting the Boston Celtics, and Borgia was working the game. Syracuse was winning big with just minutes left to play. That's when a Syracuse fan began "working" Sid Borgia. Referring to Boston coach Red Auerbach, the fan yelled, "Hey, Borgia, if you had any guts you'd call a technical on Auerbach." Blooper number one.

Blooper number two: Borgia answered. "Any time you want to try my guts, let me know."

"What about now?" the fan replied, committing the third blooper—which escalated into uncontrollable chaos when he charged onto the court and grabbed Borgia. The combative ref began throwing punches to defend himself and knocked a couple of the heckler's teeth out. That should have ended it, but it didn't.

The fan pressed charges against Borgia, and Syracuse police put out a warrant for his arrest. The testimony of a number of other fans finally got the charges dropped.

"With all the fans who always seemed to be against me when I ref'ed," Borgia said later, "I was really surprised how many were willing to go out of their way to testify for me."

Go Home, Kid—You're Too Clumsy

Perhaps the award for the biggest blooper committed by a coach goes to Notre Dame's George Keogan, who coached the Irish back in the 1940s. A player, who was 6 feet 8½ inches (2.04 meters) tall and still growing, was coming out of high school in 1942 and really wanted to go to Notre Dame. So he arranged for a tryout. When he came out on the court to show his stuff to Coach Keogan, he was wearing thick eyeglasses and sometimes appeared to have two left feet.

Keogan took one look and felt he had seen enough. He told the youngster, flat out, "You'll never be a basketball player. You're too clumsy."

An assistant coach consoled the young man, telling him not to feel bad. "Stick with it, and someday you'll be a fine player."

The player was George Mikan, and the assistant coach Ray Meyer. Not long after that, Meyer took over at DePaul, brought Mikan in, and helped make him basketball's first great center. As for Keogan, he probably spent the next four years wondering how he could have let such a good young talent go.

Glandular Goons

George Keogan wasn't the only coach to dismiss very tall, unschooled players in the 1940s. Unlike today's big guys, back then the real tall kids usually didn't play basketball until they were well into their teens. So they weren't well versed in the fundamentals of the game. That's why Keogan dismissed Mikan, and that's why a rival coach made the mistake of calling Oklahoma A&M's Bob Kurland a "glandular goon." Not only was this an unflattering remark, it wasn't even true.

Like Mikan, Bob Kurland was nearly 7 feet (2.13 meters) tall and a little awkward on the court. Had

Mikan and Kurland not persevered and become outstanding players, there might have been more bloopers made in evaluating future talent. Yet it didn't come easy for either of these big guys. They had to develop coordination, movement, quickness. In fact, Coach Meyer had Mikan box, dance, lift weights, and run with the track team.

Today's big guys come with the whole package. Can you see a David Robinson or Shaquille O'Neal, or even a Bill Russell or Wilt Chamberlain from the 1960s, begin their careers by jumping rope or running figure eights around a bunch of chairs? This was the way Mikan and Kurland started, but there had to be pioneers to show the way—especially while basketball was growing up.

Strange Franchises

In the very early days of the NBA there seemed to be a more-the-merrier philosophy when it came to the number of teams in the league. In only its fourth season (1949–50), this young league, still struggling for success, already had seventeen teams. The location of a number of them was puzzling.

At this point in its history, the NBA included the Boston Celtics, New York Knicks, Philadelphia Warriors, and Minneapolis Lakers. That much made sense, but how about the Anderson Packers, Sheboygan Redskins, Tri-Cities Blackhawks, and Waterloo Hawks? Somehow they just don't sound like professional teams with a future. They weren't.

A year later, Anderson, Waterloo, and Sheboygan were gone—so were the early franchises in Chicago, St. Louis, and Denver. Washington folded during the 1950–51 season. By year's end there were only ten teams in the NBA. Many of the early clubs simply shouldn't have entered the league. Proof of this was the fact that ten years later, in 1960–61, the number of NBA teams had decreased to eight—all solid franchises. Only then, with more great players coming in, did the league have the clout to expand slowly into other big cities.

Basketball? Oh, That's No Big Deal

Believe it or not, there was a time in the NBA's early years when basketball wasn't considered important. In 1954–55, the Syracuse Nationals and Fort Wayne Pistons met for the NBA championship. Syracuse won it in seven hard-fought games, but the Fort Wayne fans didn't get a chance to enjoy the playoffs.

The three playoff games scheduled for Fort Wayne weren't played there. They were moved to Indianapolis. Did the arena in Fort Wayne burn down? Was there a gigantic power failure, or a leak in the roof? None of the above. The NBA championships were moved to Indianapolis because a bowling tournament scheduled way in advance took precedence over the NBA. No one saw fit to move the bowling tournament to, say, a bowling alley. It stayed in the arena, while a team playing for a league championship in basketball had to move.

Even worse was what happened to the New Jersey Americans in the first year of the American Basketball Association (ABA), a league formed in 1967–68. The Americans played at the Teaneck Armory, in Teaneck, New Jersey. They were scheduled for a playoff game against the Kentucky Colonels when they learned the circus had been booked into the arena for that date. Guess who got the boot?

That's right, the basketball team. The playoff game was switched to the Commack Arena, on Long Island, New York. The team had to play in a different state, but that was only the start of their problems. To make matters worse, there hadn't been a basketball game played in the dingy old arena for years. When officials checked it out, they realized the floor was in such awful shape not even a high-school team could play there, let alone a professional team in the playoffs. There was only one thing for league officials to do—award Kentucky a victory by default. What a blooper! The New Jersey Americans didn't lose the game to the Kentucky Colonels. They lost it to the circus.

Chapter 4

Some Embarrassing Moments

In any sport, the unexpected can happen at any time and for many reasons. The result can sometimes be embarrassing, especially when a team and its individual members are playing in front of thousands of fans. Bloopers of the embarrassing kind come in many shapes and sizes. They can occur at any level of the game but are most noticeable when they happen to high-profile college teams and in the pros.

Here are a few of the most interesting super-duper bloopers—the kind that turn faces red and make people want to crawl in a hole and hide.

Let's Scrimmage the Freshmen

In the fall of 1965, Lew Alcindor, who was 7 feet 1 inch (2.16 meters) tall, began his freshman season with UCLA's Bruins. Under coach John Wooden, the team had won a pair of national championships in 1964 and 1965. As the 1965–66 season began, UCLA was again ranked number one in the country. Since freshmen couldn't play varsity ball back then, Alcindor would have to spend one season with the Bruins freshman squad.

Prior to the start of the regular season, the number-one ranked Bruin varsity got set to play a tune-up game against the young, inexperienced frosh. The arena on the UCLA campus was packed with fans wanting to see not only their varsity team, but also the talented freshman named Alcindor. What they saw turned out to be a colossal embarrassment for the varsity.

With Alcindor and fellow freshmen Lucious Allen and Lynn Shackelford showing skills beyond their years, the first-year players humbled the mighty varsity, 75–60, in a game that wasn't even close. But if the UCLA varsity had red faces, the rest of the college basketball world would soon be following suit. Once Alcindor and his fellow frosh became sophomores, they led the Bruins to three more national championships. In his three varsity years, Alcindor (who later changed his name to Kareem Abdul-Jabbar) helped his team compile an amazing 88–2 record. None of the team's wins, however, was more impressive than that easy freshman victory against their own varsity.

When Is a Game in the Bag?

Some people feel that no lead in a basketball game is really safe, but what about an 18-point lead with just 1 minute and 17 seconds remaining? Could any team blow such a big lead in just 77 seconds? Ask the players from Shasta College, of Redding, Pennsylvania. They had an 89–71 lead over Butte Community College, of Oroville, California, on January 6, 1990. Then things began going wrong.

Butte scored 8 straight points in 15 seconds, bringing the lead down to 89–79 with 1:02 left. The Shasta starters returned to the game but couldn't stop the onslaught. With 36 seconds left, the lead was down to 6 points. Seven seconds later it was just 3. Finally, a Butte player swished a 3-pointer to tie it. Incredibly, Shasta had blown an 18-point lead in 77 seconds, one of the biggest last-minute collapses in college basketball history.

But it wasn't over yet. The game went into overtime, and Shasta suddenly pulled themselves together to take a 103–92 lead with just 1:54 remaining in the extra session. Then they blew that lead! The game went into a second overtime with Butte finally winning, 116–115.

After that game, the Shasta players probably would have felt nervous even if they led by 100 points!

Don't Celebrate Yet, Coach

Coaches differ widely in their personal styles. Some are low key; they show little emotion on the bench and simply lead their teams with solid direction. Others are cheerleaders, pacing up and down, baiting officials, screaming directions to their team on every possession. Whatever works best. Yet there was one coach who probably loved his team too much, for he actually caused them to lose a game because he was so happy.

On March 2, 1988, the Fairfield (Connecticut) University Stags were playing the St. Peter's Peacocks in the first round of the Metro Atlantic Athletic Conference Tournament. St. Peter's was the heavy favorite, but Fairfield was playing a great game. In the final seconds, the Stags' Harold Brantley took a long pass and went in for a layup that gave Fairfield a 60–59 lead—and an apparent victory.

As soon as the basket went down, Fairfield coach Mitch Buonaguro went bonkers. He raced onto the court, jumped in the air, did a victory dance, and began hugging his players. He was totally ecstatic. Only there was one thing wrong. The game wasn't over.

St. Peter's coach Tom Fiore pointed out that there was still one second left and Buonaguro should be given a technical foul (which called for two shots) for running out on the court during the game. The refs agreed. Willie Haynes, of St. Peter's, made both free throws. The Peacocks then inbounded and Fairfield fouled immediately. Two more free throws made the final score 63–60.

Because of Mitch Buonaguro's uncontrollable outburst of happy emotion, the Peacocks were given a chance to score four points in the final second. It was a colossal blooper by a coach who just wanted to share a victory celebration with his team. If only he had waited one more second!

Basketball or Beachball?

When the American Basketball Association (ABA) began, in 1967, the new league looked for ways to differentiate itself from the established NBA. The ABA came up with some long-lasting innovations. They were the first pro league to use the three-point shot (today a staple of the NBA) and were the first to entertain their fans with slam-dunk contests.

One of the ABA's experimental innovations, however, turned out to be a gigantic embarrassment— at least at the beginning. League officials decided to use a red-white-and-blue basketball. They thought it would be a great marketing tool and that fans would enjoy clearly seeing the spin on the ball. Manufacturers, however, had never before made a red-white-and-blue ball. When the first group of balls came through, the players quickly found out they had two strikes against them.

The colored paint on the ball was very slippery and got worse when the players began to sweat. The ball kept squirting out of players' hands like it was greased, making the ABA game look as if it was being played by a bunch of amateurs. The problem was finally corrected, and eventually, more than half a million red-white-and-blue basketballs were sold to the public. But the first group of multicolored balls was a disaster.

The high-flying Julius Erving began his pro career in the old American Basketball Association, where the first red-white-and-blue basketballs were so slippery players couldn't hold on to them. But the ABA also started slam-dunk contests, which thrilled the fans and helped "Dr. J." become a legend.

As one ABA coach said: "The only place a ball like that belongs is on the nose of a seal."

Watch Me Dribble

Basketball, invented in 1891, didn't become an Olympic sport until 1936. That year, the summer games were held in Berlin, Germany, with twenty-two nations sending teams to vie for the gold. Games were played on an outdoor court with a surface of brick dust atop a hard layer of clay. It wasn't like playing in a gym, but it wasn't bad, either.

The United States selected players from Amateur Athletic Union teams and, as expected, dominated the competition. The gold-medal game came down to the United States and Canada. The problem was that it was raining heavily on the day of the game, yet the German organizers wouldn't postpone the match. By tip-off time, the court was covered with an inch of water.

Needless to say, it wasn't a pretty game. The tone was set early when an American player got a rebound and made a quick outlet pass to a teammate to start a fast break. The player with the ball started to dribble upcourt but didn't get very far. The first time he put the ball on the "floor" it didn't come back to him. It had gotten stuck in the mud!

The rest of the game featured passing but almost no more attempts at dribbling. The United States managed a 19–8 victory for the first Olympic basketball gold, but without the rain and mud, the scores undoubtedly would have been much higher.

Tennis, Anyone?

Basketball has always been a sport with a home-court advantage. Most teams seem to play better at home, where they are buoyed by the cheering of their fans. College and pro teams that have mediocre records on the road are often close to unbeatable when playing on the friendly hardwood of the home court. Occasionally, however, those same fans who usually root the home team to a victory pull a king-sized blooper of their own.

On January 25, 1989, Vanderbilt University was playing at home against Southeastern Conference (SEC) rival University of Florida. For most of the game, the home fans in Nashville, Tennessee, did their job, rooting loud and hard for their beloved Commodores. With just one second left, Vandy had the ball and a two-point lead over the Seminoles. The game appeared over. The Commodores had only to make an inbounds pass and the clock would run out.

Not so fast. Vandy fans had been mildly harassing Florida center Dwayne Schintzius during the entire game. Many fans had read about a pre-season incident in which Schintzius allegedly hit a fellow student with a tennis racket. Figuring the game was over, the fans decided to have some fun. They began throwing yellow tennis balls onto the court, trying to hit Schintzius.

Vandy coach C. M. Newton began waving his arms, trying to get the crowd to stop. Too late. The referee invoked a rule that imposes a technical foul on a team if its fans throw objects on the court. Since a technical in college basketball gives the opponent two shots, the Commodores were in trouble. Ironically, it was Schintzius who sank the two free throws that sent the game into overtime.

During OT it was again Schintzius who scored, this time making seven straight points to boost Florida to an 81–78 victory. What an incredible blunder by the home fans. Not only did their poor judgment cost their team a game, but it also made the object of their wrath, Schintzius, a hero.

That wasn't all. Florida went on to win the SEC championship with a 13–5 conference record. Vandy finished at 12–6. Had it not been for the fans deciding to convert a basketball game into a tennis match, the records probably would have been reversed, with the Commodores as SEC champs.

Smash the Backboard, Stop the Game

Backboard smashing is a blooper that fans love. Even the players committing this "accidental" piece of destruction seem to delight in it. The scenario is simple. A player goes up for a slam-dunk, and the entire backboard comes down with him. Either the glass shatters or the supports buckle. While it can mean a game delay of an hour or more, this wanton show of strength always charms the fans.

The first smashed backboard in the NBA occurred in 1946 and is credited to Chuck Connors, who at 6 feet 5 inches (1.96 meters) was a forward for the Celtics. The wooden backboard had splintered when Connors dunked in warmups, and a visiting rodeo provided the replacement: The arena didn't have a spare on hand. Connors, incidentally, went on to fame as an actor, starring in the popular TV western *The Rifleman* during the 1950s.

Two of the most infamous backboard busters, however, are from basketball's modern era: Darryl Dawkins and Shaquille O'Neal. Dawkins, at 6 feet 11 inches (2.11 meters) tall and 265 pounds (120 kilograms), was the center for the Philadelphia 76ers.

He dubbed himself "Chocolate Thunder" and proved it by shattering a pair of backboards twenty-two days apart back in 1979.

The first of Dawkins's pair came on November 13th, in a game against the Kansas City Kings. Dawkins flew in for a two-handed jam as the Kings' Bill Robinzine tried to guard him; the entire backboard seemed to explode, with fragments of glass going everywhere. Later, Dawkins, who loved to name his various dunks, came up with this little ditty to further joke about something that wasn't supposed to happen:

"Chocolate Thunder flyin', Robinzine cryin'
teeth shakin', glass breakin'
rump roastin', bun toastin'
wham, bam, glass breaker
I am jam."

Then, on December 5th, the 'Sixers were hosting San Antonio at the Spectrum when Dawkins went up again. This time his two-handed jam ripped the entire hoop right off the backboard. Ooops. Dawkins didn't spout poetry this time. Instead, he came out with a half-hearted apology, which was really another boast.

"I didn't mean to do it," he said. "It was the power, the Chocolate Thunder. I could feel it surging through my body, fighting to get out. I had no control."

It was this final backboard busting by Darryl Dawkins that led the NBA to install collapsible rims that give if a player hangs on to one. That might have helped Chocolate Thunder, but it still didn't prepare the NBA for a "Shaq attack."

Carrying on a Rim-Rattling Tradition

Shaquille O'Neal may be the strongest player in NBA history. At 7 feet 1 inch (2.16 meters) and 300 pounds (136 kilograms), Shaq, the center for the Los Angeles Lakers, plays an overpowering game that has reduced several backboards to ruins. Shaq originally joined the Orlando Magic in 1992 and soon after began making his reputation as a backboard blaster.

In early February of 1993, the Magic traveled to Phoenix to play the Suns. Early in the game, Shaq got the ball down low and went up for one of his patented jams. He hung on the rim for a split second, and when he let go, the backboard and rim began following him down. The bar holding the backboard had given way from the force of Shaq's slam and weight, and the entire setup sagged slowly to the floor.

"I've hit them harder than that before, a lot harder than that," Shaq said with a wink. "I was a little surprised, but when it started coming down, I ran the other way."

But Shaq wasn't through. He continued to dunk, and no one did it with more power. Then, in the second-to-last game of the year, Shaq attacked once more. Playing against the New Jersey Nets at the

Meadowlands Arena, Shaq went up for a dunk midway through the first period. He blasted the ball through, then looked up to see the structure beginning to come down on him.

This time the backboard had come loose from its top supports and was swinging downward. The 24-second clock, perched on top of the backboard, also came tumbling down and almost cracked Shaq on top of the head. Shaq just gave an "Oh, well" shrug and returned to the bench while repairs were made. For him, this kind of destruction was becoming routine.

Shaquille O'Neal goes up for one of his patented power slams in a World Championship Game against Brazil in 1994. As an NBA rookie, he perfected the "Shaq attack," which led to the destruction of several backboards.

Not even collapsible rims could withstand a Shaq attack. Maybe the NBA ought to think about making backboards out of iron to stop Shaq and the others who are sure to follow.

It's a Team Game, and Don't Forget It!

Sometimes the most valuable lessons are the toughest to learn. Every young basketball player must come to grips with the one about teamwork at some time, usually after at least one embarrassing moment.

Jim Pollard is a basketball Hall of Famer who played with the great championship Minneapolis Lakers teams of the early 1950s. Pollard was, by then, a great team player. He had learned about teamwork long before his outstanding collegiate career at Stanford University. Once he learned that lesson, he carried it with him everywhere he played.

For Pollard, the embarrassing but educational moment occurred when he was a high-school star in his home state, California. Like many high-school players, he thought he could do no wrong on a basketball court. During one game in his senior year he caught fire. Near the end of the game he already had 29 points. The school record was 30. All Pollard could see was setting a new mark. Nothing else mattered.

"I got hungry," he said. "I wanted the 31 points and took a wild shot. The coach promptly benched me with three minutes still left. I came out grumbling like a spoiled seventeen-year-old. The coach just looked at me and said, 'Jim, this is a five-man game.' He was right, and I always loved that man for setting me straight."

Jim Pollard learned the hard way what all great players learn: The team comes first.

A Strange Second Chance

Perhaps the strangest NCAA championship team in history was the University of Utah's 1944 quintet. The Utes had a young team that year, its starting five averaging only eighteen years of age. They matured quickly as the year progressed. After the regular season, however, they were passed over for the NCAA Tournament. Instead, they went to the National Invitational Tournament (NIT) in New York.

At the NIT, the Utes were beaten by Kentucky in the first round, 46–38. It looked as if their season was over. Then fate stepped in as an unexpected accident changed basketball history. The 1944 West Regional game of the NCAA Tournament was held in Kansas City. While traveling there to compete in the tourney, members of the University of Arkansas team were involved in an automobile accident. Two players were injured, and the Razorbacks were forced to withdraw. Suddenly, the NCAA needed a replacement team.

Along came Utah. The Utes were traveling home by train and had to pass through Kansas City. Since they were already in town they were asked to replace Arkansas in the tournament. Coach and players gladly obliged—with surprising results. Led by freshman Arnie Ferrin, Utah defeated Missouri and Iowa State, then headed back to New York for the NCAA championship game.

Playing against Dartmouth for the title, Utah won it in overtime, 42–40, to become the first team to win the national championship by virtue of a car accident.

A Debut to Remember

Every athlete remembers his first pro game. Whether it's a rousing success, an abject failure, or something in between, that first game is always special. Even for the greatest of players, however, it can take an unexpected turn. George Mikan's first pro game is an example.

The first of the great NBA centers, Mikan originally signed with the Chicago Gears of the National Basketball League late in the 1946 season. His first contract was for five years at $60,000, a package unheard of in those days—that's how good everyone expected Mikan to be. Indeed, he eventually led his team to the NBL title that year.

But his debut game was something else. Playing against the old Oshkosh team, Mikan got a rude awakening to the rigors of pro ball. During the game the Oshkosh center swung an elbow; on the receiving end was George Mikan's mouth. He lost four teeth—a lasting reminder of his first pro game!

Chapter 5

Where's the Ball?

In a television ad featuring Michael Jordan, now universally acclaimed as the greatest basketball player ever, the star says that twenty-seven times in his career his teammates have entrusted him with the potential game-winning shot . . . and he's missed. Of course, Jordan doesn't say how many times he's *made* the winning shot. He's one of the greatest clutch players ever to lace on a pair of sneakers, and he's not afraid to fail.

The point is that nobody's perfect. At one time or another, most players have the ball in their hands at crunch time. Some, like Jordan, want it. Others really don't but suddenly find the ultimate responsibility thrust upon them. Then it becomes a matter of coming through in the clutch or choking. When you fail, you look bad. Sometimes the blunder becomes part of the sport's folklore—a failure magnified many times because it came at a key moment, in a big game, or with the championship on the line.

Here are some of the more infamous bloopers that happened when everything was at stake, and it didn't work out for the guy with the ball.

Wrong Guy, Wrong Jersey, Wrong Team

How ironic. During the same game in which Michael Jordan began building his reputation as one of the great clutch shooters in basketball, a blooper was committed that is still talked about today. It was the 1982 national championship game between the Tar Heels of North Carolina and the Hoyas of Georgetown University.

Jordan was a freshman that year, starting as shooting guard for Coach Dean Smith. While center Patrick Ewing was the big star for Georgetown, sophomore guard Fred Brown was a regular starter who was usually expected to concentrate on defense. The game was tight and hard-fought all the way. To the delight of the 61,612 fans at the Superdome in New Orleans, the win came down to the final seconds of play.

With less than two minutes left, a Ewing jump shot closed the Carolina lead to 61–60. The Tar Heels missed their next shot, and with less than a minute left Georgetown guard "Sleepy" Floyd scored on a short jumper to give the Hoyas the lead, 62–61. Time was running out for Carolina.

The Tar Heels worked the ball slowly, hoping for a

good shot. With just 15 seconds left, the ball ended up in the hands of the freshman Jordan, and he calmly canned a 16-foot (5-meter) jumper from near the left sideline. Now Carolina had a 63–62 lead, and Georgetown had one last chance. The ball was inbounded to Fred Brown, who began working it upcourt, hoping to set up Ewing or Floyd for a last shot.

Near midcourt, Brown thought he saw teammate Floyd to his left and passed him the ball. Only it wasn't Floyd. It was North Carolina star James Worthy, who was as surprised as everyone else to receive a pass with no one around him. Brown had made a king-sized blooper. Worthy simply dribbled upcourt,

Most fans think of Michael Jordan flying in for an impossible dunk. But it was his clutch jump shot that won the 1982 NCAA championship for North Carolina, a shot that came seconds before a Georgetown player passed the ball to the wrong team, one of the most remembered bloopers ever.

where he was fouled. It didn't matter that he missed both free throws. Time ran out, and Carolina won the national championship.

As the Carolina players celebrated, Georgetown Coach John Thompson walked out on the floor and immediately hugged the disconsolate Brown. Jordan was the hero; Brown the goat. But the coach didn't blame him. It could happen to anyone. Two years later, Brown was on a Georgetown team that won the title. So he eventually dined at both ends of the table.

Pass It Here, Horse

Fred Brown is not the only player in basketball history to pass the ball to the wrong man. His gaffe was embarrassing mainly because the game was so big. A similar blunder years earlier, in 1929, was mainly funny.

The Original Celtics, perhaps the greatest of all the early pro teams, won the championship of the old American Basketball League in 1927 and 1928. The team was so much better than the opposition that, for the good of the league, the players were divided among four other teams.

Later that year, former Celtics teammates Nat Holman and "Horse" Haggerty were playing against each other on opposing teams. Holman's team was trailing by a point with six seconds left. Haggerty, now his opponent, had the ball. The wily Holman decided to try something, based on the many years the two had played together. Suddenly, he broke down court yelling, "Hey, Horse."

For a split second, Haggerty saw Holman only as his teammate and threw him a perfect lead pass; Holman cruised in to hit the winning basket. Haggerty was left with egg on his face as Holman just laughed at the success of his deception.

An Air Ball? No, the Winning Hoop

In another incredible finish in the NCAA finals, an apparent blooper turned into the winning basket. This one happened in 1983, when underdog North Carolina State was up against the powerhouse Houston Cougars, led by Hakeem Olajuwon and Clyde Drexler. Everyone thought Houston (27–2 in the regular season) would win in a walk against the Wolfpack, a team with a lackluster 20–10 record during the regular season.

But N. C. State surprised everyone, leading 33–25 at halftime. Houston came out after intermission, however, with a 15–2 run that put them in the lead. Then a Houston stall backfired, and the Wolfpack charged back. Finally the score was tied at 52-all with two minutes left. Again, Houston stalled. After the Cougars missed two free throws, N. C. State got the ball back with 44 seconds left.

Coach Jim Valvano decided to have his team opt for the last shot. They worked the ball around deliberately. Suddenly, there were just seconds left and guard Derreck Whittenburg was forced to throw up a long, off-balanced jump shot. It was apparent that the ball was going to be way short—an air ball that wouldn't reach the rim. It looked as if the game would go into overtime.

But as the ball descended, State's Lorenzo Charles suddenly leaped in the air over the Houston players, caught the ball in midflight, and slammed it through the net just as the buzzer sounded. N. C. State was the unlikely champion; Charles was the hero; and Derreck Whittenburg, who seemingly had thrown up a blooper of a shot, got credit for an assist on the winning basket.

Havlicek Stole the Ball!

When a team has just a few seconds to take a last shot, the most important thing is to get a good shot and give yourself a chance to win. Obviously, no one can make a big basket every time. A missed shot, though disappointing, is tolerable—especially if the player gets a good "look" and does his best. What hurts a team is not having enough time to put a shot up at all.

In 1965, the NBA's Eastern Conference Final was a seven-game series between the Boston Celtics and the Philadelphia 76ers. It was also a battle between the two greatest centers of the time—Bill Russell and Wilt Chamberlain—amid other great stars on each team. The hard-fought, intense series came down to a seventh and final game at Boston Garden. It was a close game all the way, with the winner undecided right down to the wire. Boston had a 110–109 lead with just seconds left, but Philly had the ball and chose to make an inbounds pass near half court.

Sixer guard Hal Greer threw the ball in. He was one of the NBA's best, and his job was simply to make a good pass to set up a final shot; it was no time for a mistake. As the players moved around to get open, Greer tossed the ball inbounds. Suddenly, Boston's John Havlicek came out of nowhere, tapped the pass away, then grabbed the ball and dribbled downcourt as the buzzer sounded. Philly never got a chance for a final shot. Greer goofed, and Havlicek's heroics were immortalized by Boston announcer Johnny Most's frantic call:

"Havlicek stole the ball! Havlicek stole the ball! Johnny Havlicek stole the ball!"

That said it all.

Bird Does It, Too

A steal similar to Havlicek's occurred in the 1987 Eastern Conference Finals between the Celtics and the Detroit Pistons. This time it was in game five. The series was tied at two games each, and if the Pistons could win the fifth game at Boston, they would head home with a chance to eliminate the Celtics.

Detroit played its heart out, and with seconds remaining they had not only a one-point lead, 107–106, but also the ball. Detroit's all-star guard, Isiah Thomas, had merely to make an inbounds pass and have a teammate run out the clock. Thomas was

The Celtics Larry Bird looks like he's headed for Bloopersville with this fall. But his incredible steal of an Isiah Thomas inbounds pass helped the Celtics win the Eastern Conference Finals from the Detroit Pistons in 1987.

standing under his own basket as his teammates scrambled for position. The veteran should have been able to pick out an open man. But he didn't.

His inbounds pass was suddenly picked off by a lunging Larry Bird. Not only did the Celtics great steal the ball, he also whirled and threw a perfect pass to a cutting Dennis Johnson, who went down the middle for the winning layup. Thomas didn't take care of the ball, and Bird made him pay. The Celts won game five, 108–107, and went on to take the series in seven.

One Missed Shot Made All the Difference

There are important shots and then there are *important* shots. Every so often a player gets an opportunity to make a shot that can win it all for his team—an important playoff series or the championship itself. It's a one-second, hit-or-miss situation with no second chance. Hero or goat. Clutch shot or blooper.

A perfect example took place in the 1962 NBA Finals between the Boston Celtics and the Los Angeles Lakers. The Celtics were trying for their fifth title in six years and fourth in a row. Led by Elgin Baylor and Jerry West, the Lakers wanted to win their first title since the team had moved from Minneapolis a year earlier.

It turned into an incredibly hard-fought battle. Despite the presence of supercenter Bill Russell and the amazing Bob Cousy at guard, the Celtics really had to fight. The Lakers won game two in Boston and then took a 2–1 lead by winning in L.A. Boston tied it, only to have the Lakers upset them again in Boston for a 3–2 lead. But the Celts played clutch ball in L.A., winning 119–105 and forcing a seventh and deciding game at the Boston Garden.

In this one, neither team would give an inch. The Lakers played fiercely, and with time running down the score was tied. L.A. had the ball and a chance to win the title. Everyone in the Boston Garden expected Baylor or West to take the last shot. Instead, the ball ended up in the hands of guard Frank Selvy. He had been one of the greatest college players of all-time, once scoring a hundred points in a game for Furman University. The final two points of those hundred had come on a last-second heave from almost midcourt. It could happen again.

Selvy had the ball and went up for a short jump shot, the kind you might make a hundred times during practice. The full house at Boston Garden held its collective breath. Could the mighty Celtics be beaten? The shot was up . . . and off the rim! Then the buzzer sounded, sending the game into overtime. The Celts regained their composure and went on to win, 110–107, for still another title.

To this day, some Laker fans wonder what would have happened if Baylor or West had taken that final shot that Selvy missed. Had he made it, he'd still be remembered as one of the great heroes in Lakers history. Alas, no one makes them all. A matter of inches can change everything.

What Foul?

The 1993–94 NBA playoffs produced not one, but two last-second situations involving the New York Knicks. The Knicks were trying to win their first league crown since 1973. Their first test came in the Eastern Conference semifinals against the Chicago Bulls. The Bulls were three-time defending NBA champs, but they were playing without superstar Michael Jordan, who had gone into temporary retirement.

By season's end, many fans felt the Bulls were playing the best basketball in the league. The two archrivals split the first four games. Now came the all-important game five at Madison Square Garden in New York. If the Bulls could win it, they would take a 3–2 lead back to Chicago, where they would have a good chance to close out the Knicks in six.

Like so many games between these two teams, this one went down to the wire. With 7.6 seconds left, the Knicks trailed by a point, 86–85. But the New Yorkers had the ball and a chance to make the last shot. Guard John Starks began driving to the hoop but was cut off by a Chicago defender. With the seconds ticking away, Starks shoveled a pass back to fellow guard Hubert Davis, who was standing just inside the three-point line.

Only 2.1 seconds remained when Davis went up for a jumper that could win or lose the game. With the Bulls' star Scottie Pippen leaping at him, Davis launched the shot. It went off the right side of the rim as the capacity crowd groaned in dismay. That was before they heard referee Hue Hollins blow his whistle.

Hollins had called a foul on Pippen, saying he had made contact with Davis's hand after he had launched the shot. Pippen and the rest of the Bulls erupted, claiming the contact had been incidental after the shot, didn't alter the shot, and was no foul. But Hollins persisted. Davis stepped up to the line and made amends for missing the big shot by canning both free throws to give the Knicks an 87–86 victory and a 3–2 lead in the series.

"That call might be made one time in a hundred," said the Bulls' center Luc Longley, echoing the sentiment of the entire Chicago team. The Bulls did win game six, only to have the Knicks take the seventh and deciding game. Had Hollins not blown his whistle, however, the entire face of the playoffs might have changed.

So who committed the blooper? Davis by missing the shot? Pippen by brushing the shooter's hand after the ball was released? Or referee Hollins by calling a foul that shouldn't have been called? It's your choice.

No Foul Here

The Knicks finally made it to the championship round in the 1993–94 NBA playoffs. They would be meeting the Houston Rockets in what the press billed as a clash of top centers—Patrick Ewing of New York and Hakeem Olajuwon of Houston. The series, however, included much more than that. Every game was an epic battle, and the defenses kept the scores below 100 points.

After five games, the Knicks had a 3–2 lead. Even though game six was at the Summit Arena in Houston, the Rockets knew their backs were up against the wall. If the Knicks won, it would be all over. Not surprisingly, the two teams battled hard once more, the score staying close almost all the way. Again, it came down to the final seconds.

With less than a minute remaining, the Rockets held a very slim, 84–82, lead. Houston had the ball and tried to work for the good shot. When they got it to Olajuwon, he was quickly fouled. He sank both free throws to put his club up 86–82 with 39.3 seconds left. The Knicks, however, wouldn't quit. An Anthony Mason jumper at the 32-second mark cut the lead to 86–84. Then a Houston miss gave the Knicks the ball again, this time with just 8 seconds left. The Knicks would have a chance to tie or win it.

As the clock ticked down, the Knicks looked for a last shot. They couldn't go inside to Ewing, and John Starks ended up with the ball behind the three-point line with very little time. Just before the buzzer sounded, Starks went up with a three-point try. If he made it, the Knicks would win the championship. If he missed, there would have to be a seventh and deciding game.

Then, just before he released the ball, Hakeem Olajuwon came rushing toward him and leaped in the air. Reaching as high as he possibly could, Olajuwon barely ticked the ball as it left Starks's hand. That slight deflection, however, was enough to send the ball off its mark, and it bounced away just as the buzzer sounded. The Rockets had won.

Because Olajuwon had tipped the ball and not touched Starks there was no foul. Houston went on to win the championship in seven games. As for the Knicks, they had come close. The game-winning shot was in the air but didn't go in.

A block or a blooper? What if Starks had fired a split second sooner? Then Olajuwon couldn't have reached it. Would Starks have been a hero?

Chapter 6

Bloopers, Bloopers Everywhere

So many strange and unusual things have happened in the sport of basketball over the years that it's impossible to include all of them in a single book. But let's try to honor as many as we can. This chapter is a potpourri of things that happened on the hardwood that will amaze and entertain you, make you laugh, and occasionally make you feel a little sad. For bloopers, though sometimes funny to watch, do not make the player happy. In one way or another, he has failed or perhaps made himself look silly. Even if it takes just a second or two to happen, the blooper is not something an athlete wants to remember.

But every sport has a lighter side, and athletes are only human. So appreciate bloopers for what they are—moments that are sometimes amusing and even unbelievable.

How's This for a Dunk?

The slam dunk is often just what the name implies. The ball is slammed—hard—through the hoop. Players like Darryl Dawkins and Shaquille O'Neal have shattered backboards and taken down hoops with their explosive jams. Other players fly under the hoop so quickly when they dunk that the ball hits them in the head as it comes through the net.

Despite all the great NBA slammers and jammers, perhaps two of the wildest dunks happened in the college ranks. In both cases the players probably wished they had taken a conventional layup and just banked the ball in. Both events happened in 1976–77, the first season the dunk was again permissible in college basketball after having been outlawed in 1967–68.

Because there had been no dunking for a decade, players went all out to show what they could do. A little-known player named Claude "Snowflake" English, who played at tiny Christian College of the Southwest, flew in for a jam. The ball rocketed through the hoop, then hit English on the head and opened a large gash that needed several stitches to close. Ouch!

But Wiley Peck, of Mississippi State, went English one better. On a breakaway, Peck decided to show everyone just how hard he could dunk. He slammed the ball through the hoop with all the strength he could muster. It must have been considerable, because when the ball came through the net it struck

Peck in the face. He crumpled to the floor, where he lay unconscious for a full two minutes.

Hey, What Happened to Our Team?

During the 1966–67 season, the Philadelphia 76ers had the best team in the NBA. In fact, they were one of the best of all time. Led by center Wilt Chamberlain, guard Hal Greer, and forwards Chet Walker and Billy Cunningham, the Sixers finished the regular season with the best record to date in NBA history, 68–13. They then raced through the playoffs, defeating the San Francisco Warriors in five games for the NBA championship.

You would think the core of a great team would remain in place for years, but somebody goofed. Just six years later, in 1972–73, the Philadelphia 76ers established another record, one that still stands. It was a record for futility. The team combined an NBA worst-ever mark of 9–73. Those Sixers featured the likes of Fred Carter, Manny Leaks, Fred Boyd, Dal Sclueter, and a host of others who came and went during the season.

Who goofed? To let a team go from record-breaking best to record-breaking worst in six years is a king-sized blooper if there ever was one!

Dinner for Two

There's no question that Charles Barkley, of the Houston Rockets, is an NBA all-time great. Since joining the Philadelphia 76ers out of Auburn

University in 1984–85, "Sir Charles" has left his mark on the league. Despite being listed in the NBA guide at 6 feet 6 inches (1.98 meters) and 252 pounds (114 kilograms), there are those who say that Barkley is closer to 6 feet 4½ inches (1.94 meters). Regardless of his height, he plays power forward, bumping heads with players much taller than he is.

In 1986–87 Barkley became the shortest player in NBA history to win a rebounding title as he grabbed 14.6 caroms per game. Yet there was a time when Charles was on his way to committing a huge blooper—one that could have cost him his

Future Hall of Famer Charles Barkley looks lean and mean while playing for the Phoenix Suns in 1993. But as a collegiate star at Auburn years earlier, Barkley had a great appetite for pizza that caused his weight to soar and almost cost him a pro career.

NBA career. The culprit wasn't his game; it was his appetite.

When he played at Auburn, Charles was known as the "round mound of rebound." He got that nickname as much for his girth as for his rebounding skills. Barkley admits that back then he didn't take the game as seriously as he does now. As his weight ballooned to more than 300 pounds (136 kilograms), Charles accumulated a number of unflattering nicknames: Tons of Fun, Food World, the Goodtime Blimp, the Bread Truck, the Crisco Kid, Fat Boy, and the Leaning Tower of Pizza.

There was a good reason for that last one. There was a pizza parlor not far from his apartment on the Auburn campus. Every night, Barkley would dial the number and say these three words:

"This is Charles."

A short time later, two large pizzas would be delivered to his room, and Barkley would have his evening snack—dinner for two. Fortunately, Charles took stock of his future and realized that his wallet would become a good deal fatter if the rest of him shrank a few sizes. The rest, as they say, is history.

Change the Rules!

Today, most of the best college basketball teams get a chance to compete in the NCAA Tournament and win the national championship. It's not unusual for four or five teams from the same conference (the Big Ten, Big East, or Atlantic Coast Conference, for example) to all get bids to the big show. Unfortunately, it wasn't always that way.

There was a time when only a single team could represent certain conferences—the team that won the conference tournament at the end of the regular season. So there were many deserving teams that didn't get a chance to compete for the NCAA title. Perhaps the most deserving team that should have gone but did not was the 1974 University of Maryland Terrapins.

Coach Lefty Dreisell's Terps had three All American–caliber players in guard John Lucas, forward Len Elmore, and center Tom McMillen. Early in the season the Terps met defending champion UCLA. Led by center Bill Walton, the Bruins were in the midst of an 88-game winning streak, the greatest in collegiate history. Against Maryland, it almost ended. Maryland trailed 65–64 in the closing seconds when John Lucas went up for a shot that could have won it. Fortunately for UCLA, Dave Meyers blocked the try and the Bruins remained unbeaten.

Then, in the Atlantic Coast Conference (ACC) championship game, the Terps went up against once-beaten North Carolina State. It turned out to be one of the greatest college games ever played. N. C. State finally won it, 103–100, to earn a bid to the NCAA Tourney. Maryland finished its season at 23–5 and was ranked number four in the country in both the Associated Press and United Press final polls. Yet because of an illogical rule, which was eventually changed, they were denied a bid to the tourney.

A Rain Out . . . in Basketball!

This one is hard to believe. On January 28, 1961, a game between West Hazelton High School and McAdoo High in Pennsylvania had to be stopped at halftime. West Hazelton was leading, 31–29, in an exciting contest. The problem was the floor.

It seems someone had opened a few windows at the top of the gym. The cold air from above combined with the heat in the gym and caused condensation on the floor. The players were beginning to slip and slide, and for their safety the game had to be called off. It wasn't officially ruled a "rain out," but it may as well have been.

Chaminade—Sounds Like a Fruit Drink

The University of Virginia had one of the top collegiate teams in the country during the 1981–82 season. Led by center Ralph Sampson, who was 7 feet, 4 inches (2.24 meters) tall, the Cavaliers were considered potential national champions. In December, the unbeaten Cavaliers traveled to Hawaii to participate in an annual Christmas tournament; they were, of course, the favorites.

Virginia's first game was against the local entry— Chaminade University of Honolulu. It was supposed to be a laugher, but no one told that to the Chaminade players. They came out with fire in their eyes and surprised the entire basketball world by upsetting Sampson and Virginia, 77–72.

Talk about a blooper. The powerful Cavaliers, a

team that would wind up ranked third in the country and with Sampson the Player of the Year, had just lost to a school with a total enrollment of 850 students and a seven-year-old basketball program. Who said Chaminade sounds like lemonade?

The Opposite of Hot

Every once in a while nearly every basketball player has a night he wants to remember. He can't miss. He's on fire. He's in the zone. He can feel it. He wants the ball and ends up with a great game.

But what about the opposite, when the game feels like one big blooper? Nothing works. Nothing goes right, and he can't find the basket. That happens, too—sometimes to outstanding players. For years, the record for shooting futility in a game was 15: that's 15 straight misses with no baskets made. Seven different players have had this type of blooper-filled night. In fact, Howie Dallmar, of the old Philadelphia Warriors, had two of them.

Then, on December 27, 1991, that record was broken by an unlikely player. The Golden State Warriors were playing at San Antonio that night in a game that would go into overtime. For the length of the entire game, Tim Hardaway, Golden State's point guard, was ice cold. He tried. Oh, how he tried. He took jump shots, drove the lane, fired three-pointers. Nothing would fall through. By game's end, Hardaway had shot the basketball 17 times and hit . . . nothing! His 0–17 set a new record.

What made it more amazing was that Hardaway was, and is, one of the league's top players. That season, he was sixth in the league in scoring with a 23.4 per-game average, finished third in assists with 10.0 per game, and made the All-NBA second team. Yet for one night he looked as bad as any recreational clunker who just can't buy a basket, no matter how hard he tries.

Let's Try That Free Throw Again

There have been great free throwers in the NBA, and there have been notoriously poor ones. No player likes missing a free throw with the game on the line. If a player who shoots maybe 85 percent misses a big one, people will say he choked. If a player who shoots 50 percent or worse misses, oh, well, he rarely makes them anyway. Yet in the eyes of many people, consistently missing free throws is a blooper. Nobody is guarding you. You're close to the basket, and you can shoot the ball any way you want.

Some players, however, seem to unravel completely on the foul line. During his rookie year with the Boston Celtics in 1971, Garfield Smith stepped to the free-throw line in a three-to-make-two bonus situation. Smith not only missed all three, he didn't even come close. He had thrown up three straight airballs. Try it yourself. That's pretty hard to do.

But Smith never had much luck at the line. For the season, he made just 39.3 percent of his free-throw tries. A year later, still playing for the Celtics in a limited role, Smith bungled and blooped even more from the charity stripe. He made just 6 of 31 free-throw attempts for an anemic 19.4 percent. Bet the opposing players just loved fouling him.

Dudley Didn't Do Right

Chris Dudley is known as a defensive center—a big guy who'll clog the middle and rebound. He's never been known for his scoring prowess and has even less proficiency at the free-throw line. Playing for the Cleveland Cavaliers in 1988–89, his second season in the league, Dudley went to the free-throw line in a game against Washington and had everyone shaking their heads in wonder.

Since he was fouled in the act of shooting, Dudley was awarded two free throws. He missed both, but the ref's whistle blew. One of the Washington players was in the lane too soon. Dudley was awarded another shot—and missed. Again, the ref sounded his whistle. Another lane violation. Dudley had a fourth chance, and the same thing happened. He missed the shot, but a Bullets' player was in the lane too soon for a third time.

So Dudley stepped up to the line for a fifth try. The Washington players hung back, not wanting yet another violation. Sure enough, Dudley clunked another one off the rim. Five straight free throws; five misses. Maybe they should have let him dunk.

Wilt's Foul-Line Frustration

Free-throw shooting was the only weakness in the great Wilt Chamberlain's game. Considered by many the most talented center ever, Wilt once averaged 50 points a game for an entire season—a record that will never be broken. He also played more than 1,000 games and never once fouled out. In addition, he is one of the NBA's all-time leading scorers and its all-time rebounding champ.

Still considered by many the greatest center who ever played, Wilt Chamberlain had one glaring weakness. He couldn't shoot free throws. He tried every style possible, even the old underhand shown here. One night Wilt topped himself by missing all ten free throws he attempted.

But, for all of his accomplishments on the hardwood, Wilt couldn't shoot free throws. He tried shooting them every way imaginable. Overhand, underhand, standing off center on the foul line, standing a bit behind the foul line. He ended his great career shooting only 51.1 percent from the charity stripe. There were even a number of years during his long career that he was below 50 percent.

The pattern for Wilt's frustration was set as early as his second season. Playing for the Philadelphia Warriors against the Detroit Pistons on November 4, 1960, Wilt went to the foul line ten times. He missed every one of them! His 0–10 still stands as the worst free throw game any NBA player has ever had.

Ironically, Wilt's greatest game was also his greatest night from the foul line. Playing for the Warriors against the New York Knicks on March 2, 1962, Wilt scored an incredible total of 100 points, including 28 of 32 free throws. That, in itself, might have been even more amazing than the 100 points.

A Non-Contact Sport

Somebody goofed when they tabbed basketball a "non-contact" sport. It was rough in the early years, and it's rough today. The contact is not programmed into the rules, as it is with football or hockey, and some fouls are called when one player just barely touches another. But when big, strong men are contesting for rebounds and loose balls or battling for position, it can get pretty bruising.

Are hard contact and injuries considered basketball bloopers? In some cases, perhaps. The great George Mikan, basketball's first dominant big man, played just seven full seasons and part of two others as a pro, yet his medical report makes it sound as if he played defensive tackle for the Chicago Bears.

Over his NNL/NBA career, Mikan had 166 stitches taken to close various wounds. He also had two broken legs, a broken foot, a broken wrist, a broken nose, three broken fingers, and some teeth knocked out. One time, big George heard an opponent claiming that he (Mikan) was "getting away with murder" under the boards.

Enraged, big George is said to have ripped off his own shirt to reveal a mass of fresh black-and-blue welts on his chest and back. "Ask them what they think these are," he growled. "Birth marks?"

Oh No, Not the Trophy

The first-ever NCAA post-season tournament was held back in 1939. There was just an eight-team field chosen that year, and the championship game came down to a contest between the University of Oregon and Ohio State University. The tourney didn't officially determine the national champion back then, but both finalists wanted to win it very badly.

Only 5,000 fans attended the first title game, which was held on March 27th, at Patton Gym on the campus of Northwestern University in Evanston, Illinois. Oregon's front line was nicknamed "The Tall

Firs," but the driving force behind the Ducks was hustling 5-foot 8-inch (1.73-meter) guard Bobby Anet. He scored 10 points in Oregon's 46–33 victory; he also did something he hadn't planned.

During a tense part of the game, Anet charged full speed after a loose ball. He couldn't quite reach it, and his momentum carried him off the court and into a table set a few feet away. When officials surveyed the damage, they saw that Anet had not only crashed into the table, he also had broken the championship trophy that had been made especially for the first-ever winning team.

Although the trophy would have to be repaired, the Ducks were happy to have won it anyway. Anet's unintentional blooper was quickly forgiven.

This Game Looks Easy

The New York Knicks' great center Patrick Ewing looks as if he was born on a basketball court. His energy, work ethic, and love of the game must have been developed since early childhood, right? Not quite.

Born in Kingston, Jamaica, Patrick didn't arrive in the United States until 1975, when he was twelve years old. That's when he saw basketball for the first time. Soon after arriving in Cambridge, Massachusetts, with his family, he saw a bunch of kids playing basketball. He thought it looked easy.

"I could see the object was to put the ball in the basket," Ewing said. "Then I tried it and found the game was much more difficult than I ever imagined."

Ewing wouldn't make that mistake again. Hard work finally led him to Georgetown University in Washington, D.C. As a freshman in 1982, he led the Hoyas all the way to the national championship game against North Carolina. Then, in the opening minutes of the game, Ewing's exuberance and determination led to a strange occurrence that some people felt might have cost the Hoyas the ball game.

Trying to establish a defensive presence in the middle, Ewing went after the first four Carolina shots. He swatted all of them away before the ball even reached the basket. There was just one problem. In each case, the ball was already on a downward trajectory. Instead of getting credit for a blocked shot, Ewing was called for goaltending four straight times. Because of that, North Carolina had an 8–0 lead, and they hadn't even put the ball in the basket once.

Carolina wound up winning by a single point. What might have happened if Patrick Ewing hadn't gone block crazy in those opening minutes?

Just One More Point

Former Old Dominion star Anne Donovan was an outstanding collegiate player. In 1983, she won the Naismith Award as College Player of the Year. Donovan played 136 games for Old Dominion and scored 2,719 points, which gave her a career scoring average of 19.9926 points per game. It rounds off to

20 points, but there would be no need to round off if Donovan had scored one more point. Just one more hoop, a single free throw, and her average would have been an even 20.

How many times did she go over her career in her mind and think about that one point? A missed free throw, a blown layup, a short uncontested jumper, any of probably a hundred or more shots that could have gone in but didn't—one less blooper anywhere along the way.

What a Way to Start . . . and End

No team likes it when things are going badly. Losing streaks can be painful. They sometimes even seem to feed on themselves: a series of mistakes by one player, then another; a blooper here, a blooper there. Just when things seem to be going right, they suddenly go wrong.

Perhaps the worst kind of losing streak occurs at the beginning of a season. After all, once it starts badly, the road back is long and difficult. During the 1988–89 season the Miami Heat were an expansion franchise playing their first NBA game. They must have gotten the hint then that life in the NBA wouldn't be a cakewalk. The Heat set a record for early-season blunders by losing their first 17 games in a row. They finished the year at 15–67.

The 1981–82 Cleveland Cavaliers also struggled, compiling a 15–48 record with 19 games left. They must have reasoned that if they could win maybe 10 of their last 19 they could at least salvage a 25–57 record, which wouldn't be the worst in the league. Plus it would be something to build on for the next season.

It didn't work out that way. The Cavs suddenly went into their worst tailspin of the season, stumbling and bumbling and finding a way to lose the final 19 games: a record for end-of-the-season futility. Like the Heat, the disappointed Cavs finished with an anemic 15–67 record.

Can't Anyone Here Score a Point?

On February 4, 1987, the Sacramento Kings took the court against the Los Angeles Lakers at the Lakers' home arena, the Great Western Forum. The Kings probably didn't feel too good about their chances. After all, the Lakers had the best record in the NBA and would eventually take all the kudos that year. In contrast, the Kings were in the midst of another losing season. Facing the likes of Magic Johnson, Kareem Abdul-Jabbar, James Worthy, and the rest of the Lakers didn't boost their confidence, but none of the Kings was prepared for what happened.

The Lakers came out fast, as usual, pushing the ball upcourt with their patented fast break, driving the lanes, or giving the ball to Abdul-Jabbar for his unstoppable sky hook. In the meantime, the Kings were playing a king-sized game of blooper ball. They were throwing up bricks.

Unbelievable as it sounds for a professional basketball team, the Kings went a full 9 minutes and 6 seconds without scoring a single point. By that time, the Lakers had a 29–0 lead and had put the game on ice. When the quarter ended, Los Angeles had a 40–4 advantage, and all the Sacramento points came on free throws. The team had a collective 0–18 from the field.

In fact, the Kings didn't score their first field goal until early in the second quarter, after they had missed 21 straight shots. That isn't exactly what's meant by "keeping it close."

How About Some Defense?

For nine seasons, from 1981–82 to 1989–90, Doug Moe was the coach of the Denver Nuggets. During that time, the Nuggets produced seven winning seasons. Moe's philosophy was to shoot quickly and score—no milking the 24-second clock, just put the ball up as soon as you can. As a result, his clubs were among the highest scoring in the NBA every year. On the defensive end, however, they sometimes forgot to show up, and the Nuggets often gave up the most points in the league.

Things got especially bad on November 30, 1983, when Moe's Nuggets were taking on the Portland Trail Blazers. On that night, the Denver defense was worse than usual and the Blazers were running through them, meeting no resistance.

With a little more than a minute remaining in the

game, someone pointed out that the Blazers were getting close to scoring a team-record 150 points. His squad already hopelessly behind, Moe decided to commit an intentional blooper that he thought might wake the Nuggets up. It was a gamble that ultimately cost him dearly.

He called a timeout and told his players, "Let them have it. . . . You understand what I'm saying, don't you?"

The coach basically ordered his team to stop playing defense. The Blazers went out and quickly got five uncontested layups to win the game, 156–116. The Nuggets' defense didn't really improve after that game, and for his not-so-subtle suggestion, Coach Moe was fined five thousand dollars and suspended for two games.

This Team Wouldn't Fold, Until . . .

When center Bill Walton arrived at UCLA in the fall of 1971, the Bruins had their logical successor to Lew Alcindor, who had led the team to 71 straight wins and 3 NCAA titles. Sure enough, the 6-foot, 11-inch (2.11-meter) redhead was all his press clippings said he was. Once he began playing with the varsity squad in the 1972–73 season, Walton and a superior supporting team began winning. They were unbeaten for two straight years and added another pair of national championships to the Bruins' growing ledger.

By the time Walton was a senior, in 1974–75, it

was widely assumed that the Bruins would continue their impressive winning streak, which had reached a record 88 straight games in the latter part of the regular season. That's when the Bruins met the Fighting Irish of Notre Dame. The Irish were a good team, but not in UCLA's class.

Most of the game went according to script. With just three minutes left, the Bruins had a 70–59 lead. But even the best can lose it. All of a sudden, UCLA couldn't buy a basket, couldn't make a free throw. Notre Dame began closing the gap. Not even the great Walton could stem the tide. Notre Dame scored the last 12 points, miraculously winning the game, 71–70, and ending the longest winning streak in college basketball history.

Everyone has to lose, but it was hard to believe that the seemingly invincible UCLA would do a disappearing act in the last three minutes. The blooper of blowing that game seemed to set a pattern, because the Bruins lost two more before the season ended; then they lost to North Carolina State in the semifinals of the NCAA Tournament. To this day, Bill Walton still finds it hard to believe his team lost those four games.

"After our 88-game win streak was broken," Walton says, "we lost something. We ended up losing four games to teams we should have beaten. We should have won 105 games in a row."

And Finally . . . Nickname Bloopers

Basketball franchises have always moved from city to city. In some relocations, the team nickname changes; in others, it doesn't. For instance, when the Philadelphia Warriors moved to the West Coast they became the Golden State Warriors; when the Syracuse Nationals moved to Philly, the nickname was changed to the Philadelphia 76ers.

Occasionally when a team moves, the special significance of a nickname in one city is lost in another. Two examples come to mind. The Minneapolis Lakers had gotten their name for a good reason. The state of Minnesota has more than 15,000 lakes, which are a major tourist attraction. When the team moved west, the name Lakers was retained, even though there is not a single natural lake in and around the city of Los Angeles.

Similarly, when the city of New Orleans received an NBA franchise, the team was appropriately nicknamed the Jazz. It fit. New Orleans was one of the birthplaces of American jazz, and New Orleans jazz is a specific style of that musical genre. When the team moved to Utah, they kept the nickname. Utah, however, has absolutely nothing to do with the history of jazz music. Seems like someone should have thought about that. Then again, with good sense and strict logic, there wouldn't be any bloopers for us to enjoy.

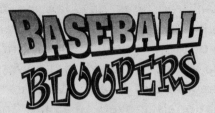